The Edvard Munch TAROT

for relationships

By: *Red Orchid Publishing*

Melanny Eva Henson

Introduction

When I begin a new card divination project, I look for gaps in what is available to learners. What challenges do readers face? I ask myself, and is there a way to aid or assist that process that isn't currently available? So for quite a while it has occurred to me that a tarot deck designed specifically for relationships could meet learners' needs on multiple levels. It could be particularly valuable to those new to tarot, as it would teach them to read the energy through one particular lens. One challenge I identified is that the broad perimeters of possible interpretations for any one card was enough to make a person's head spin. Deducing the process down to one type of interpretation could be especially valuable in the beginning journey of learning all those subtle distinctions. I sat with this idea for about a year and waited for the right artwork to find me.

The other reason I thought this deck should exist is the disproportionate number of readings dedicated to relationships. Of the readings I give, I would say slightly more than 50% are inquiring on this topic alone. So a deck designed specifically for that purpose would be valuable to professional readers as well. Although tarot readers typically understand the cards well, the customer often finds the images confusing and alienating. Indeed, when I give paid readings, I work almost exclusively with Anna K tarot cards because the imagery is accessible to the lay person. I show them the cards and explain the interpretation, and the imagery on the cards aid heavily in their understanding of my interpretation. That particular deck is exceptional for that express purpose, and though I have no personal connection to the creator, I have no qualms about inadvertently promoting it as a good example. So, I felt that a relationship deck with accessible imagery that could be more easily understood by the lay person would be a valuable tool for professionals, customers, and beginning readers alike.

Lastly, if you are purchasing this deck to read for yourself, I also created this deck for you. The tenuous nature of relationships and our deep, primal need for social connection and acceptance make navigating relationships one of the greatest challenges of our life journey. Sometimes I get the sense that people are becoming more self-centered and that as a society our value systems have shifted away from community and towards ourselves. In cases where we are being exploited or suppressed for the health of the community, this shift can be not only beneficial, but crucial. Generally speaking, however, this cultural shift is often toxic, and has inspired many people to go running to their tarot cards in order to navigate the pain and isolation they have experienced from another's selfish impulses. I feel you. I have been there, and I wrote my interpretations with you in mind.

Channeling Edvard Munch

I stumbled upon Munch's work when I began a journaling project, The Tarot Journal for Healing Heartbreak. I felt Munch embraced the theme of relationships in his work with greater internalization and vulnerability than other painters, and I fell in love with the subjective quality of his expressionist work. My previous deck, Art History Tarot for Past Lives, featured 78 historical painters, and though I felt a vague connection to them and felt the fortification of their spirits with the project, I did not develop any kind of personal repertoire with them.

Even though I am a psychic medium, as a general rule I don't channel famous people. So I was not expecting to channel or connect with Edvard Munch as I pored over his paintings, constructing my journal, and then eventually continuing on to the creation of this deck. But one day, I received a clear vision of his face, and I knew he was visiting. I engaged and talked to him. Apparently, he had been lurking around for months. He possessed the resolve and healed energy of someone who had gone towards the light, not much at all like the anguished soul he had been during his lifetime, but grandiose and angelic with the powers of knowing that come when you return home and regain your perspective.

I worked up the courage to ask him if I had known him in that life. I felt he affirmed yes. I didn't ask who I had been, preferring not to know. I think it's likely I was someone not known to history, (he had many lovers). As I combed through his biography, I felt my own fiery personality was similar to Tulla, but when I came across Eva Mudocci, my heart did stop a little. Back in 2011, I had given myself the middle name "Eva" as part of my pen name, without really knowing why. Also, Eva had two children: Isobel and Kai. I have three children, two named Elizabeth and Kira. However, I have never felt particularly drawn to violins, (Mudocci was a professional violinist) and I saw no physical resemblance between us, so I remained uncertain. Upon my third revision of the deck, I scoured the Internet for a better photograph of Eva's full length portrait, only to discover that this painting is displayed at a museum in Northfield, Minnesota, an hour and a half's drive from my home. For a cosmic moment, I felt magically connected to my work, and fortified in my task. Although I remain unsure of who I could have been if I was indeed connected to Munch in another lifetime, I find it is questions like these that keep life interesting and engage the imagination with meaningful possibilities

In the first draft of this introduction, I wrote about my experience "working" with the spirit of Munch, but upon further reflection, I think it's best to keep that experience personal rather than make claims that are inadvertently speaking for someone who is no longer here to speak for himself. I am not attached to the idea that I conversed with Munch's spirit, and I happily accept alternative interpretations of my experience, such as that I have an overactive imagination (I certainly do) that helped propel me forward to this project's completion. I don't question my mediumship abilities, but I also prefer to find value in the subjective nature of such experiences. Our perceptions and narrations remain mystical precisely because they cannot be proven and this is the fodder for true magic as we strive for meaning against a life of struggle and adversity.

Deconstructing Gender in Readings

A lot of Munch's paintings (though not all) feature a heterosexual dynamic. His relationships with women preoccupied his mind and influenced his work heavily. Therefore, this deck often showcases a male/female dynamic. However, I don't consider this deck hetero-normative. Rather than seeing a literal male and female in these cards, I challenge you to think in terms of masculine and feminine energy. A relationship between two men, (or two women, or two non-binary people) still contains a mixture of what we deem "masculine" and "feminine" energy. At first glance, this might appear sexist or marginalizing to think this way. I would argue that it is our insistence that someone embody or reflect masculine and/or feminine qualities that contributes to the toxicity of sexism, and not those qualities themselves. For example, a woman who is excessively feminine or reflects all our society deems feminine is not inherently wrong in her existence as long as these qualities are innate to her being. It is the woman who performs femininity, who rejects the masculine parts of her self (and almost any woman with depth possesses those) who has embraced the toxicity thrust upon her sex and reinforced a culture intent on consuming her.

So when you draw a card featuring a man and woman, ask yourself: who is the man here, and who is the woman? Just because you are asking about a heterosexual couple, that doesn't mean that the man in the painting is the man, and the woman is the woman. Instead, who is exuding the male energy in the situation? (Ex: aggression, initiation, pursuit, self-service, leadership) and who is exuding female energy? (Ex: passivity, creativity, self-sacrifice, submission). These energies are sometimes mixed in the paintings within this project, with the woman as the aggressor (consider the seven of swords in this deck; the woman is clearly the male energy in that painting). The original Rider-Waite Tarot partially functions through a paradigm of masculine and feminine, and this deck aligns with that tradition. Again, I don't reinforce this dichotomy as an ideal, (I'm not saying men are aggressive and women are passive) but rather I employ this distinction for the sake of reading the energies. It isn't wrong to acknowledge male energy or female energy as an objective observation. It is wrong to expect someone to exude an energy they don't naturally possess, and it is wrong to punish them (consciously or subconsciously) for not meeting a cultural expectation. I believe that in order for our society to adequately heal, we must reject our societal expectations.

With all that said, there are certainly LGBTQ decks on the market that better fulfill a gender-fluid need, should you have such a need, and it is understandable and acceptable to me if you don't feel this deck meets your personal framework. This deck highlights masculine and feminine energy, and that might function better for some more than others.

Unique Qualities of This Deck

There are a few aspects to this deck that are unique in comparison to traditional tarot decks.

1- Orientation

Because the compositional framework for Munch's art includes a varieties of shapes, it occurred to me it would be better to include both portrait and landscape orientation for the cards. The key question arises: How do I read reversals with landscape cards? When you turn the card over, if the text appears on the right, it is upright. If it appears on the left, it is reversed. Of course, you have the option of not reading reversals at all.

Text on Right     **Text on Left**

2- The Pages as Children

For the purposes of this deck, the Pages have been re-imagined to reflect psychoanalytic aspects to a person's psyche in order to gain greater insight into the dynamics at play within the relationship. The pages can indicate a literal child in the relationship, or one or both party's formative childhood experiences that have shaped their personality and worldview today.

3- The Knights

The Knights are not as much male figures in this deck as they are symbols of particular relationship events that establish, fortify, or alter the qualities of the relationship. Both male and female figures appear in the Knight cards to indicate this card applies to two parties and the unique dynamic between them.

Sample Spread

For more spread ideas, check out:

The Tarot Journal
for
Healing Heartbreak

Beginning

0-The Fool

General Reading:

The Fool card is about new beginnings and marks a new journey, as the Fool travels through the remaining twenty-one cards of the major arcana and gathers new experiences for learning. As we are all on the personal journey of the Fool, acquiring new knowledge and gaining wisdom, this card reflects a much deeper interpretation than general foolishness. This is the card of the learner, the adventurer, and marks the beginning of a new path.

"Red Virginia Creeper" 1898-1900

How Someone Sees You

For how someone sees you, this card usually means you are seen as naive or perhaps adventurous. If you see someone through the lens of Fool energy, you see someone acquiring new experiences and taking in their environment with the excitement of a child. The world is full of possibilities for you, and you have not given up on believing an exciting life is within your grasp. You crave excitement and hold a healthy curiosity about the world.

Future Event or Outcome

As a future event or outcome in a relationship, this card means one of two things: 1) The two of you will start on a new journey together. The rules, dynamics and expectations that were in place before will be revised or changed entirely. 2) One of you will make a major life decision that takes you on a new journey. You may or may not be together.

Divining the Art

Although at first glance you might think the word "Creeper" refers to the unnerving human figure in the foreground of the painting, it's actually referring to climbing vines that commonly grow alongside buildings in Virginia. The blood representing vines on the house in the background of this piece asks you to observe what bloody truth lays behind you. The life you leave behind you has some public stains. But the figure in the foreground of this image does not look ashamed. He stares ahead unabashed. The Munch Fool indicates someone with a past, but who is ready to look to their future. They are likely ready for a new relationship that will enhance their quality of life. Perhaps the figure represents you or the other party in your relationship

Manifestation

I-Magician

General Reading:

The Magician is masterfully resourceful. He/She not only possesses magic, but is capable of great tangible manifestations. He/She can also be incredibly cunning and if crossed, a formidable enemy. When reversed, this card amounts to manipulation, gaslighting, and subtle abuse. Upright, He/She is capable of astounding greatness.

How Someone Sees You

For how someone sees you, this card usually means you are seen as a resourceful and powerful person. You are not seen as a victim. It's possible the person perceiving you is quite jealous of your talents and gifts. They might struggle to trust you because they sense an immense inherent power within you.

Future Event or Outcome

As an outcome card, you can expect tangible results. Your mind will be clear and you will have spiritual insights that will guide you towards concrete steps to take for your desired outcome.

"Julius Meier Graefe" 1885

Divining the Art

Julius Meier Graefe was a key writer for the Impressionist movement, and an artist in his own right. Writers and artists often encapsulate Magician energy, as they take abstract ideas, thoughts and feelings and transform them into money. Julius' stovepipe hat is reflective of the performing magician that says, "Look at me. Give your attention here, and expect a grand performance." The Munch Magician denotes a grand, theatrical person in your life whose creative talents have monetary value.

Wise Woman

II- High Priestess

General Reading:

The High Priestess is the embodiment of the Divine Feminine. She is quiet and observant, at times the keeper of secrets. She is not quiet by submission, but through her gained wisdom. She has learned to observe and reflect before taking action. She is slow to speak as a protective measure, and conversely, withholds empty words of affirmation or praise expected by others. She knows the empty gratuity that may pacify them will only drain her energy.

How Someone Sees You

If someone sees you as the High Priestess, they see you as evolved, self-assured, contained, balanced and empowered. You may be sought out as a source of wisdom or perhaps considered a resource to greater knowledge. You are seen as spiritual and as someone with considerable depth. You may also be seen as secretive or someone who does not reveal all their cards or wear their heart on their sleeve.

Future Event or Outcome

As a future event, the High Priestess indicates a secret. This secret is the elephant in the room for one party, while the other party is kept in the dark. If this card is paired with The Moon anywhere in the spread, this indicates the secret will be revealed.

"The Brooch" 1903

Divining the Art

This portrait is of Eva Mudocci, lover and longtime friend of Edvard Munch. Mudocci (given surname at birth was Muddock) was a professional violinist, lesbian partner to pianist Bella Edwards, and met Munch in Paris in 1903, the same year as this portrait. Most of Munch's lithographs during this period were on paper, but there were a few exceptions (like this one) where the lithograph was done on stone. The brooch (the focal point of this painting) was a gift from art historian Jens Thiis two years prior. Munch said Eva had "the eyes of a thousand years." Munch's High Priestess is a woman of depth, wisdom, and secretive allure.

Fertile Woman

III- The Empress

General Reading:

The Empress represents fertility and all creativity. When she appears, a creation wants to come forth, whether that be a project, song, a painting, or a literal child. The Spirit World is tapping you on the shoulder so you will heed the whispers of manifestation. The Empress creates and is above all, a creator. With the Empress, you can be certain a window to the soul will be opened.

How Someone Sees You

If someone sees you as the Empress, they could simply be very sexually attracted to you. You light within them the burning passion that has continued humanity. If you are a woman, they might visualize you as the mother of their children. But if they are not a family oriented person at this time, they will still feel an undeniable drive to connect with you sexually.

Future Event or Outcome

As an outcome, expect a creation. This could be as literal as a pregnancy and child, or this could be a metaphor for art that you either create together, or that is inspired by one party and created by the other. If you are indeed pregnant, this is a good omen for a healthy birth.

"Madonna" 1895

Divining the Art

Is this woman rising upright before you or lying beneath you? Her intense feminine draw is tempered by her surrendering body language and relaxed face. Though the features of her breasts are subtly portrayed, her sexual availability (perhaps relenting?) is unmistakable. Her right hand disappears into the ether while her left arm hides ready in the shadows, giving us the impression that her submissive state could be a ruse. Her angelic halo indicates sainthood, and yet its red color connects us to the blood of the world and to the flesh It is her sexuality that connects us to the Divine. With Munch's Empress, you may feel you have access to her body, and yet she hides the more valuable aspects of herself from your grasp. Will those who want her have the discernment to notice her true value, or will they be distracted by aesthetics? This Empress is an attractive woman with more to offer than pleasures of the flesh.

Patriarch

IV- The Emperor

General Reading:

Emperor energy reflects the power of the world. Political influence, standing in the community, and considerable wealth are the trifecta of qualities encompassed by the Emperor card. This card typically represents someone with considerable worldly power. When reversed, abuse of power is certain. Upright, he can be a protective ally.

"Rue Lafayette" 1891

How Someone Sees You

If someone sees you as the Emperor, they see you as in charge, both generally and specifically. You have
the reigns in most situations and you also have the power to do considerable destruction. You likely make this person feel vulnerable when they are around you. Whether you are more educated, have more secure employment, have more status at your job, or earn a better income, their own insecurities are being provoked by your accomplishments.

Divining the Art

Munch's Emperor overlooks the streets of Paris, knee bent comfortably as he looks down upon the world and reflects over all he has accomplished. It appears he has borrowed our Magician's hat. Perhaps he possesses the resourceful powers of the Magician, or perhaps he has simply convinced others he deserves to wear it. This Emperor will show you his true colors as he climbs the ladder of success. The intoxication of power and influence will reveal his true heart. Does he recognize his good fortune, or does he firmly believe he has earned it, blind to the broken backs that ensured his success? Look for humility to know you've found a good man.

Future Event or Outcome

As a future event or outcome in a relationship, this card indicates an increase in worldly power. One or both of you are currently moving up in the world, and this new status will likely test the relationship. If reversed, stay acutely observant of red flags that indicate egoism, superiority, or power plays with money.

Wedding

V- The Hierophant

"Dance of Life" 1899-1900

General Reading:

The Hierophant (the Pope card) indicates religious tradition, and will often indicate a public wedding in a relationship reading. Generally, this card is about any established cultural expectations.

How Someone Sees You

This person sees you as someone who follows tradition and tries to meet the expectations and ideals of your surrounding culture. They might see you as religious or as someone who is acutely aware of how things are "supposed" to be done.

Future Event or Outcome

As a future event this would indicate a wedding or a ceremony that is part of a long-standing tradition. It could also indicate attending a church.

Divining the Art

The most interesting aspect of this wedding scene is that our central figures are not actually the bride and groom. The marriage couple is often thought to be the couple in the left background. We also have two female voyeurs to the central couple's happiness: a woman dressed in white, assumed to be a young maid, and the woman in black is likely an older woman. A subtle criticism of marriage is portrayed here: it is the couple who have not yet committed who inspire the attention and envy of the onlookers. This card can be a reminder that weddings offer security, but perhaps not joy or excitement. The maid looks on longingly, her hands slightly reaching towards the couple. She desires what she is seeing. A tall flower leans towards her, indicative of the beautiful future that will bloom for her. The older woman has hands clasped, resigned. She understands this romantic journey will have ups and downs and won't offer her the keys to a fulfilling life. Also note the grotesque man hassling the woman in the right background. Where are you in this painting?

Lovers

VI- The Lovers

"The Lovers" 1913

General Reading:

Lovers can be literal and indicate a sexual relationship, or more broadly it means a choice. Even when the card indicates a physical relationship, there are deep spiritual aspects at play, most likely a soul contract is commencing or being negotiated on the earth plane.

How Someone Sees You

This person can't stop thinking about you. When separated, they will likely dream about you. There is something compelling about you that arrests them. This likely makes them very uncomfortable. Even if this person acts as though they don't care, you can be assured that the feelings run deep on a subconscious level. If this person has left you, that decision is embedded in their psyche and they reflect on that choice in their quieter moments.

Future Event or Outcome

If this card appears in the outcome position, it would indicate a continued relationship or a reunion. The critical choice between you has not yet been made, but will be made at some point in the future.

Divining the Art

The male in this painting is nearly expressionless. He looks away from his partner while she succumbs to the intense throes of passion. He seems almost disconnected from his partner as she covers his third eye with her hand. Munch's Lovers asks you to consider who is enjoying this relationship, and who is behaving like an outside observer. Someone feels spiritually oppressed by this union, though this could be based on fears of commitment and not necessarily validated by the reality of the situation. It could be that the feelings of oppression are indeed valid and based on the confines of a relationship that won't allow the individual to grow.

Drive

VII- The Chariot

General Reading:

The Chariot is about crusading energy, charging forth into the life you desire. Often portrayed with a dark and light horse, the symbolism refers to making a decision of which direction to go, or perhaps managing two forces simultaneously in order to keep moving forward. Look for the competing energies in your life. You've got this!

"Horse Team in Snow" 1923

How Someone Sees You

If someone sees you as the Chariot, they see a driven, determined person who doesn't back down from adversity. This quality is viewed in a positive light, and they admire your tenacity. You are seen as a leader, crusader, and a capable person. Don't be surprised if this person expects you to juggle many things at once-- they feel you can handle it!

Future Event or Outcome

Expect a decision to be made that will alter the course of your relationship. This can be anywhere from parting ways and pursuing different paths to one party making a cross-country move so you can be together. It is not necessarily a breakup card, but you can expect something to change dramatically.

Divining the Art

The ubiquitous snow in Munch's Chariot indicates a period of struggle and compounding adversity as a decision is about to be made. The driver is not holding the reigns of his horse team, indicating that the driving desires of the situation will lead the decision to be made, rather than calculated analysis or thorough reflection. He is not bundled in clothing against the elements, suggesting the forces against you are manageable at this time. Although cut off from the card space, this original image of this painting reveals a friendly dog playfully cutting off the horse team. A surprise element will enter this situation; expect a moment of delight as passions drive your relationship forward.

Divorce

VIII- Justice

General Reading:

The Justice card is ultimately about fairness and receiving your just due. More often than not, literal court cases are reflected in this card. In relationships, this card's presence indicates a legal divorce. If you are wondering if a divorce is indeed forthcoming, this card affirms that reality. Legal filings can be expected.

"Self Portrait with Tulla Larsen" 1905

How Someone Sees You

For how someone sees you, the Justice card means you are seen as a just and fair person. You have a clear moral compass and defined barriers for yourself between right and wrong. You act according to your established internalized morality. This person recognizes this quality in you. Beneficially, you are seen as having strong moral standards, and so their view of you is positive. But the caveat to this perspective is that the person you are asking about could be willing to exploit your sense of right or wrong, since he/she can accurately predict your reaction in certain situations. Consider this person's character for this interpretation.

Future Event or Outcome

As an outcome, this card will indicate either: 1) Legal proceedings or 2) Due karma. Your question should help determine which of these is the correct interpretation. For relationship questions, this card usually means divorce, but when paired with positive relationship cards such as four of wands or two of cups, it would mean a wrong being made right.

Divining the Art

This fascinating painting was sawed in half by Munch himself. Munch's relationship with Tulla Larsen lasted only four years. Though he never married, Tulla Larsen was the only woman he has been photographed with. She fought with him frequently over wanting a commitment, something he was determined to withhold from her (and every other woman, for that matter). She chased him with the same stubborn passion that he had for staying single. At the culmination of their relationship, Munch lost a finger by gunshot during an argument. Most likely, Tulla shot him, since he never talked about it, and he clearly felt responsible for the conflict. Afterwards, he sawed this painting in half. Is the man in the background an aspect of Munch himself? His guilt? Or perhaps the demon that tortures him and instills the doubts about commitment? The woman is miserable in this painting, and Munch indeed made Tulla miserable. The redheaded woman featured predominantly in Munch's paintings, suggesting a great loss he never expressed verbally, and a situation he was determined to never make right. Munch's Justice brings the reckoning that is owed due to someone's selfishness.

Withdrawal

IX- The Hermit

"Melancholy" 1894

General Reading:

The Hermit indicates personal growth gained through withdrawal. Although someone may seem absent at this time, he or she is working through their feelings, connecting to the higher self, and evolving into a stronger individual.

How Someone Sees You

If you are seen as the Hermit, they might see you as someone who withdraws into your own personal cocoon fairly regularly. It is also possible that you are seen as wise, and a spiritual resource to this person, as they see you as someone who withdraws to meditate and makes sound decisions.

Future Event or Outcome

As an outcome, expect someone in the relationship to need to some space to come to terms with their reality. This typically does not indicate a permanent withdrawal from the relationship, but someone who will have greater clarity when they resurface.

Divining the Art

The figure in this painting is clearly sad, (the name of the piece is "Melancholy" after all) so Munch's Hermit is withdrawing due to some discontent in life. The waters are calm. An empty boat beckons. The figures standing on the dock are ignored. Our Hermit sits languidly, barricaded by large shore stones. The natural world will protect you at this time as you go inward. Conflicts and stress can wait as you take time to reflect and take stock of what you have going for you at this time. There is time and space for meditation. You may fear there will be fires you won't be prepared to put out if you take time for yourself, but that's an illusion.

Fate

X- Wheel of Fortune

General Reading:

The Wheel indicates the passage of time, and the inevitability of change. Typically, this card brings good luck and what has up till now been a treacherous and not-so-ideal situation will make a sudden shift into better times. If everything has been going great, you can expect a shift that will shake up your reality, but more often than not, this change brings a positive angle to your situation.

How Someone Sees You

If someone sees you as the Wheel, this would indicate a subconscious attachment to you. The Wheel is about the passage of time and the ups and downs of life, so if someone is viewing you through this lens, then that would mean they see you as part of their life during the ups and downs, that their connection to you is fixed, forged by fate or perhaps a soul contract agreed upon before your perspective incarnations. They may not be aware that they see you this way, but their behavior and orientation towards you will provide clues that their attachment to you goes deep.

Future Event or Outcome

As a future event or outcome, expect the unexpected. A great shift is about to commence and a new reality is in the early stages of development. Whatever wheel has been set in motion in your life, there will be no stopping it now.

"The Kiss" 1896-97

Divining the Art

The unclothed figures in this painting express a certain level of vulnerability. Comfortable in their shared embrace, they cling to each other with idealized romanticism. Lights from an apartment building across the way shine in the background; the world gazes on. A nearby houseplant eclipses the window, as the earth gives its nod of approval. Munch's Wheel card assures us that life will be good. The dictates of our soul paths have led us here to this moment. The two of you are meant to be, and even if separated, will still belong to and be meant for each other.

Wound

XI- Strength

General Reading:

The Strength card is ultimately about healing, recover,y and persevering. It also indicates a deep wound that affects the situation. When this card appears, healing is assured.

"love and Pain" 1893-1895

How Someone Sees You

If someone sees you as the Strength card, they see you as someone who has overcome great challenges and pain in your life. You are someone who has taken a beating and gotten back up. They see you as perhaps vulnerable, but able to recover and heal your pain rather than someone who would take out your pain on others.

Future Event or Outcome

As a future event, this could indicate someone will get hurt deeply. However, if a deep wound is already present in the relationship, as an outcome card this would indicate the journey towards healing will commence.

Divining the Art

An alternate title for this painting is "Vampire," giving the painting an edge not apparent with its original title. The idea that she may be biting his neck and sucking his blood makes this painting more about victimization rather than a heart-torn embrace between combating lovers. Munch's Strength card could be about the deep pain being inflicted by one party onto another for selfish purposes. Or it could indicate the awkward and fumbling love extended that will begin the healing process between the two. Ask yourself if the other party you are inquiring about has the emotional capacity to self reflect and change. Your answer to that question will tell you which title for this card is most appropriate. That dark shadow looming behind the couple reflects the truth.

Silence

XII- The Hanged Man

General Reading:

The Hanged Man denotes a suspension of time. We are upside down and fixed in a state that impedes our ability to move forward. A relationship falls silent as one or both parties rethink their level of commitment to the pairing.

How Someone Sees You

If someone sees you as the Hanged Man, they see you as someone incapable of advancing. Perhaps they believe you don't have viable career opportunities, or maybe they feel you are too fixated on a past relationship or lost love in order to begin a stable future with someone new. You appear stuck to them in some way. They do not feel responsible for your fixed state and instead hold you entirely responsible for your predicament.

Future Event or Outcome

As an outcome, expect a period of withdrawal or silence between you. One or both of you will stop communicating for a time. Little will be resolved during this reprieve, and spiritual growth will be minimal if at all.

"Despair" 1892

Divining the Art

It's difficult to look at this painting on not notice the same red and yellow striped sky from "The Scream." The bridge with background pedestrians is the same as well. Our figure is not as near the brink of madness in this painting, however. Instead, he is more withdrawn, sad and resigned. Munch's Hanged Man has gone quiet, but his angst is markedly absent of drama. Expect the dual frustrations of silence and stagnating growth.

Change

XIII- Death

General Reading:

The Death card brings death to the life we have known. A trans-formative change occurs, and the life we were living fades as we begin a new cycle. This card can but rarely indicates physical death. A relationship will either restructure or end.

How Someone Sees You

The other person is so afraid of what a relationship with you would mean that they can't see past their own fear to evaluate you accurately. They see you as bringing about monumental changes in their life due to the deeper feelings of commitment they hold toward you.

Future Event or Outcome

This relationship will end or there will be a radically new dynamic within the relationship. The relationship the two of you once had is over.

Divining the Art

This painting depicts woman in three stages: Maiden, Mother and Crone. Munch's death card marks a major life transition for a woman. The Maiden is dreaming, but faceless and without an established identity. Our Mother is nude, deduced down to her fertility and sexual attractiveness. Our crone seems vaguely depressed, as though a life committed to patriarchal values has left her unfulfilled. One interesting aspect to this painting is Munch including himself in this scene. His presence seems misplaced and excessive to me. His head is bowed in disappointment or sadness. Perhaps someone in your life is insisting on making your own radical changes about them, shifting the focus on how your journey will be impacting their own life. Don't be afraid to disappoint others as you honor your own Goddess path. Your change is all part of a natural cycle that you cannot alter. You can only adjust your perspective and attitude towards these cycles and changes of life.

Dynamic

XIV- Temperance

General Reading:

The Temperance card instills balance in a situation. Needs are being met. Extremes in circumstances and emotions have dwindled, and peace can find its way into our life. Temperance is about moderation, and the comfort of a predictable dynamic.

"Man and Woman" 1915

How Someone Sees You

If someone sees you as the Temperance card, they see you as someone who is balanced, who doesn't succumb to impulses or acts rashly. You are seen as someone wise and self-controlled enough to avoid addictions and you are relatively balanced emotionally, especially when compared to other people in this person's life. Expect this person to lean on you for stability.

Future Event or Outcome

As a future event or outcome, you can expect this relationship to settle into a familiar harmony and supportive routine. There will eventually be an equal amount of give and take in this relationship if it doesn't exist already. You can expect this person to care about your feelings and dreams.

Divining the Art

The splendid color palette combined with the captivating geometry of this painting reflects a vivacious and exciting dynamic between this couple. Although the man is turned away from the woman in profile, the viewer gets the sense he is heading towards her. She fastens a button unconsciously and stares forward with confidence. He has not yet given her a reason not to trust him. She holds optimism for their future. With Munch's Temperance, you can expect the traditional balance and tranquility of this major arcana, but colored with a streak of excitement as well.

Devil

XV- The Devil

General Reading:

The Devil in tarot refers to imbalance, often unhealthy excess. This is the card of sexual kinks, alcoholism, drug abuse, gambling addiction and obsession. At times this energy can serve a particular purpose, such as obsession up to the fulfillment of a short term project. Typically, however, this card is a warning sign that unhealthy behavior needs acknowledging.

How Someone Sees You

For how someone sees you this card could mean that they see you as having some sort of unhealthy addiction. It could also mean that you are the addiction: they are sexually interested in you in an unhealthy way that serves their selfish purposes but does not honor your spiritual being.

Future Event or Outcome

As an outcome, I would be concerned in drawing this card. It means that you or your partner's propensity for imbalance or excess is so severe that it will likely tarnish the relationship. Watch out for the one who talks incessantly of sexual fantasies: that person is all about their own desires and needs and has little concern for yours.

"Self-Portrait in Hell" 1903

Divining the Art

This satirical self portrait leads us to wonder whether Munch was aiming at humor or self depreciation. A large shadow figure looms behind him. Does it represent the demon who tormented him in life, or is this an aspect of the shadow self? The figure appears to be touching Munch's shoulders, connected to him in an unsettling manner. His expression is quite resigned: he has accepted the darker aspects of the self as fixed rather than a challenge to be mastered. Watch out for the person who isn't preoccupied with spiritual growth.

Separation

XVI- The Tower

"Separation" 1896

General Reading:

The Tower card indicates an event that is both out of your control and that brings upheaval to a situation. Reversed, this card refers to a Tower event that occurs slowly over time. Upright, the event is swift and often unforeseen.

How Someone Sees You

If someone sees you as the Tower, that means they are terrified of you or how a relationship with you would require them to change. It's likely that these feelings are unfair or shaped by their own fears and shortcomings.

Future Event or Outcome

As a future event or outcome, the Tower card means you should expect the relationship to crumble to an extent. Some relationships do rebuild after a tower event, but this event will shake the foundation for at least a period of time.

Divining the Art

The heartache in this painting is palpable. The faceless figure turning away from the man indicates a woman unknowable. Perhaps he has refused to truly see her or maybe she has worn a mask. Her hair trails back and connects to him, indicating the soul ties between them. Certainly, she was his lover.. He clutches his heart in acute pain, and we get the distinct sense that this relationship is over. Her absence has distorted the natural world around him, warping his perception of the world. An enormous red flower in the foreground rests just below his heart like a pool of blood. Her dress melds into the sand, as she walks toward the shore. He is of land, and she of sea. He is focused on the material world while she bathes in her emotions. The clear connection between them may draw them back together at some point in the future.

Guidance

XVII- The Star

"Starry Night" 1893

General Reading:

The Star card assures you that you are being guided. You are aligning with your higher purpose, and there are clear signs from your guides and the universe that you are on your predetermined path.

How Someone Sees You

If someone sees you as the Star, they see a clearly defined future with you. This person probably feels deeply attached to you. They are hoping you will be part of their ideal narrative. If you don't return these feelings, it's best to communicate honestly.

Future Event or Outcome

As a future event or outcome, you can expect a clear sign from the universe. If you are questioning or doubting this relationship and unsure what your next move should be, there will be indications, whisperings, and/or signs to lead you in the right direction. You can trust your gut in this situation.

Divining the Art

This is the lesser known "Starry Night" painting by Munch. I chose it for its raw connection to nature. We are submerged in the natural environment here, without the lights of society to distract from what's truly within us. The tall, rounded precipice with its straight white line is rather yonic, an unconscious emergence of Mother Goddess, who makes no threats of violence nor demands loyalty, but extends love and support unconditionally and without recognition. The constellations reflect off the water in exaggerated lines, alluding to our emotions' ability to highlight important truths. Don't disparage yourself over your feelings, because those feelings provide tremendous insight for your life. The lovely hints of purple and green throughout this painting remind us that when we close our eyes in meditations, there is more to see than the black of night.

Intuition

XVIII- The Moon

"Moonlight" 1895

General Reading:

The Moon card refers to the subconscious, the unknown and the unseen. It is the card of secrets, but it also carries the deeper aspects of intuition, psychic insight, and spiritual knowing.

How Someone Sees You

For how someone sees you, this card has a few different interpretations. They might see you as spiritually gifted. It could also mean they can't figure you out or you strike them as secretive. The last interpretation is that they haven't yet figured out what they think of you. Read their cues to figure out which interpretation fits best.

Future Event or Outcome

As a future event or outcome, expect a secret to be revealed. Whatever is being hidden will eventually be uncovered, often happening as the moon waxes.

Divining the Art

The reflection of moonlight on the water in this painting lines up perfectly with the stone landing near the shore. It's a beautiful metaphor for spiritual wisdom finding a channel to manifest in the physical world. The power of three is encompassed by the three trees in this painting (a common trope for Munch). They are somewhat phallic and could represent either the Holy trinity or the triple goddess (depending on your mood). A dark, anthropomorphic cloud looms near the full moon. Is it Goddess? Is it the embodiment of the unknown? Is it a thought form? This opaque confusion will not eclipse the truth. In time, what is unknown shall be known.

Joy

XIX- The Sun

"The Sun" 1909

General Reading:

The Sun card in tarot is a positive omen, bringing joy, renewal and hope. The universe supports your chosen path and will fortify your journey into greater satisfaction.

How Someone Sees You

If someone sees you as the Sun, you are the light in their day. Just being around you fills them with joy and optimism, and their overall health and being improves in your presence.

Future Event or Outcome

This card brings good news for the future. Expect positive changes, joy, happiness, and fulfillment. This card sometimes indicates pregnancy or a child. The sun has come out and shines merrily over this relationship. Expect your partnership to go public.

Divining the Art

The Sun is considered one of the greatest achievements of modern mural paintings. Munch was hospitalized with a nervous breakdown in 1908. When he emerged from care, he felt somewhat healed. His artistic style shifted some, most noticeably away from darker psychological themes, and he soon after painted The Sun. The mural is an exquisite composition of light and color, and emanates the peace and joy Munch grappled for in this phase of his life. Munch's Sun brings hope and joy after the storms of life. You've been through a lot, but now you've reached a better phase.

Awakening

XX- Judgment

"Peace and the Rainbow" 1918

General Reading:

The Judgment card has heavy spiritual connotations. It encapsulates the Resurrection or Second Coming of Christ. All that has past is brought forward to be judged and dealt with. This card brings a personal reckoning, inspired by a spiritual awakening.

How Someone Sees You

If someone is viewing you through the lens of Judgment, their perception of you has shifted dramatically over time. They now see you with more clarity and accuracy, and if you have felt misunderstood by this person in the past, you can expect that to change.

Future Event or Outcome

As a future event or outcome, you can expect a personal revelation to awaken within you. As you puzzle with the complexities of your relationship, an A-ha moment will arrive, the rubble of confusion will fall away, and the truth will shine like a promising rainbow in your mind and heart. You will know what to do.

Divining the Art

The scene in "Peace and the Rainbow" features worn and weakening figures lying across each others on the ledge of barren mountain. Their arms outstretch hopefully to the distance where a jagged white landscape waits beneath a rainbow. Within the white ledges, human-like figures appear, perhaps spirits or angels waiting on the other side of the earthly existence. The title leads us to believe these humans have reached the end of a long journey and can now at last cross over into the peaceful spirit world. All that is true comes forth into the light in this moment. With Munch's Judgment, expect clarity and truth to emerge, and with this forthcoming internalized honesty, peace will be yours.

World

XXI- The World

General Reading:

The World card is a fortuitous omen. The material world lays at your feet, and all its offerings are available to you. You are connected to the earth and wander among others with ease. Social structures and nature both bend to your will.

How Someone Sees You

If someone sees you as the World card, they see you as a valuable person. Perhaps they see you as trophy material if they were to win your heart. Or they might feel that they could put your perceived wealth to good use. Ultimately, they see you as someone that the world values.

Future Event or Outcome

As a future event or outcome in a relationship, expect a positive turn of events with this person, one that strengthens your public bond and inspires the envy of others.

Divining the Art

Munch's World in this painting is fantastical and cheery, complete with a pink road. The vibrancy of color in this composition depicts an idyllic and nearly fairytale-like scene. The sky is clear and bright, and the world is a pleasant place. Whatever strange, amorphous mound lurks to this woman's left, it doesn't seem to phase her. Abstract concerns and anxieties have been set aside. The darkness of the world sings out only in minor keys as the pleasures of the world reign dominant in this woman's experience. Expect life to go your way for a change. Even the street complements your frock today.

Hope

Ace of Cups

General Reading:

Aces in tarot refer to root energy. They typically indicate the potential of a situation rather than a manifestation. The Ace of Cups refers to potential emotion, specifically positive emotions. There is definitely hope for happiness and joy in this situation.

When reversed, beware the false heart.

"Waves Against the Shore" 1911

How Someone Sees You

If someone sees you as the Ace of Cups, they think you are a loving person with a lot to give. They might even see you as having a limitless supply of loving energy to give others. They certainly feel you are kind and generally a good person with a selfless heart.

Future Event or Outcome

As a future event or outcome in a relationship, this card means you can expect an outpouring of love to occur. This could possibly come from you, but with other positive surrounding cards in the spread, it means your own cup will be filled, and the potential outpouring will likely come from the person you are asking about. Expect a direct love confessional.

Divining the Art

The dawn of a new day always brings fresh energy and a bit of hope. In the water's reflection, the sun is exaggerated and its light beautifully accents the waves of the sea. The potential for hope in your life right now is great. The disconnected sun rays from the body of the sun denote the expansion of the sun's energy. The trellises of hope in your own situation are so powerful and far reaching, their connectedness to source may not be readily apparent, but if you observe your situation closely, that connection can be felt. The shores of your life are cast in pinks and purples right now. Whatever you are hoping for, give yourself permission to believe in it!

Commitment

2 of Cups

General Reading:

The Two of Cups is the card of commitment. Two parties enter an agreement that is mutually beneficial and acceptable to both of them. There is typically a balanced and happy dynamic between the two people.

No reversed interpretation.

"Two People on the Way to the Forest" 1894

How Someone Sees You

If someone sees you as the Two of Cups, they see you as a person of your word. When you agree to do something, you do it, and this person knows they can depend on you. Alternatively, this card could mean that they feel personally committed to you, or they see you as someone they would be wise to enter into a commitment with.

Divining the Art

These two figures head into the thick of the trees together. They have made a conscious decision to walk the same path, and to face life's adversities and unknowns together. The blues and pinks on the path reflect a whimsical partnership with fluttery feelings between them. A small, reflective pond rests to their side right before they embark on this journey together. Are you making the right choice? The pond seems to be asking. Have you looked clearly at the situation? When you envision the two of you on your journey together, does it feel right?

Future Event or Outcome

As a future event or outcome in a relationship, you can expect an agreement, most likely publicly acknowledged, where the two of you will be together. You can expect a formal commitment on social media, a proposal, or marriage.

Friendship

3 of Cups

General Reading:

The Three of Cups is a jubilant card of camaraderie and socialization. When this card appears, you can expect a friendship to develop alongside enjoyable social engagements. A friend group emerges that marks a pleasant phase of your life.

Reversed, this card can mean an expedition, or an end to a friendship.

"Girls on a Bridge" 1900

How Someone Sees You

For how someone sees you, this card would mean that they see you as the life of the party, that you seem to be adept socially and not only good with people, but fun to be around as well. They might view you as a partier.

Divining the Art

Three young girls gaze merrily over a bridge at the still waters below. They are comfortable in each other's presence. At this time, the sky is blue and inviting, and the calmness of the water offers a clear reflection of life. Friendship and socializing is at the center of your life and partnership right now. Drink in these good times! This is what life is all about.

Future Event or Outcome

As a future event or outcome in a relationship, expect an outing together that will build memories you reflect back upon for years to come.

Discontent

4 of Cups

General Reading:

The four of cups refers to an offer that you are pondering. Discontent is often felt with this card, as none of the options seem that appealing and you aren't eager to align yourself with any decision at this time. Whatever is being offered to you in this relationship is not palatable.

Reversed, this card means look to the horizon for a new relationship.

How Someone Sees You

For how someone sees you, this card would mean they see you as an option. Commitment and partnership are both far from their mind concerning you. You can take heart in the knowledge that this person isn't satisfied with anyone, and that the discontent they feel toward you isn't personal, but a reflection of their own lack of maturity.

Future Event or Outcome

As a future event or outcome in a relationship, I would expect this partnership to go stale. One or both of you withdraws due to a general dissatisfaction with life in general and doesn't feel ready to go forward with a relationship.

"Head by Head" 1905

Divining the Art

Neither partner in this composition looks particularly happy. The male seems distracted and consumed with his own thoughts, turning away from his partner. She clutches him, but no longer looks towards him as she seems to sense his evasion. Emotionally, this couple is disconnected. The blue swirls that circle the couple hint at water, a common divinatory symbol for emotions. We can't seem to get out of our heads to be present in this relationship. Black, scar-like tattoos trailing the woman's arm hint that she is someone who has been deeply hurt and is now looking for solace in another's arms. The yellow hues in the skin tone of both partners could imply illness, a metaphor for the mental illness that obstructs the connection between this couple.

Disappointment

5 of Cups

General Reading:

The five of cups is a card of acute disappointment, as our attention is fixed on the what is lost and what we retain fades into the background of our reality.

Reversed, expect news, or an alliance, or important information about your ancestry.

How Someone Sees You

For how someone sees you, they feel that on some level they have lost you, and they grieve that loss. Alternatively, they might view you as pessimistic.

Future Event or Outcome

As a future event or outcome in a relationship, you can expect to be disappointed on some level. This comes dramatically, as you are fed unrealistic expectations that are never realized. When the truth hits, it will hurt. Take stock of what you still have to find solace.

Divining the Art

The woman in this painting attempts to process her sorrow, indicated by her hunched posture and free flowing hair. Notice that much of this scene looks and feels incomplete; blank spaces peek through the water and there are stones that are traced yet not fully formed. She is losing her grip on reality as she succumbs to the intense depravity of her emotional pain. The green boulder sits large before her, fully formed, and offering her support. What is the green boulder for you in this situation?

Childhood

6 of Cups

General Reading:

The Six of Cups is the card of nostalgia, childhood memories, and looking to the past. This card can sometimes indicate a past life relationship, when paired with the Wheel of Fortune.

Reversed, this card advises you to look ahead to the future, and to not focus on the past.

"Bathing Boys" 1897

How Someone Sees You

For how someone sees you, the Six of Cups means they see you as having a playful and adolescent spirit. If you have a shared past, then they have favorable views of you based on happy memories they shared with you. Those memories have value to them. There is a familial bond between you.

Future Event or Outcome

As a future event or outcome in a relationship, this card means one of two things: 1) The two of you will start on a new journey together. The rules, dynamics and expectations that were in place before will be revised or changed entirely. 2) One of you will make a major life decision that takes you on a new journey. You may or may not be together.

Divining the Art

This beautiful composition powerfully captures the joys of childhood. The nudity in this painting is innocent and represents freedom and being unencumbered by society's demands and expectations. Note the taller/older boy who appears to be standing in his own niche on the shore. A bright blue stream leads to him, and there's a direct path from his nook to the broader water. The joys of today are feeding your spirit and will give you strength and endurance as you re-enter the stresses of the world. This is a time of making memories. Feel free to be your true self and strip away all that others said you should be. The world is ripe for an authentic version of you!

Fantasy

7 of Cups

"Meeting on the Shore" 1896

General Reading:

The Seven of Cups is about passions and choices, sometimes marked by fantasy. This card typically indicates indecision and/or not seeing situations as they truly are.

When reversed, expect intense desire.

How Someone Sees You

For how someone sees you, this card means they view you with rose-colored glasses and are blind to your faults, for now.

Future Event or Outcome

As a future event or outcome in a relationship, this card lacks a concrete resolution. Expect a period of indecision and playful fantasies that lead nowhere for a while.

Divining the Art

Notice that the water in this painting gets darker as it gets closer to shore. This is an inverse to reality, where water gets darker in perceived color as it gets deeper. The transposition probably highlights the intense feelings and desires of the two figures in the painting, as this mermaid brings powerful emotions to the surface. He props his face in his hands and gazes at her dreamily. He sits on the stable shore, lined with a thick fence of impenetrable trees, represents the male space of the material world. And the mermaid in the sea represents female space, where mysteries of nature are buried and true spirituality is hidden from view. Between these worlds, they meet, but he sees only what he wants to see. The unfinished form of stones on the shore indicate he isn't seeing his surroundings clearly. Does he think this woman is a mermaid, or does he see a fish that looks like a woman? She has almost no face and gazes back with a vacant fish eye. Expect someone to look past the true you in order to see what they want to see.

Moving On

8 of Cups

General Reading:

The Eight of Cups involves taking stock of everything you have invested in something you thought you wanted, and then making the conscious decision to leave it behind you. It is the card of moving on.

Reversed, this card means great joy or a feast. Expect what you walked away from to return. Attempts to leave will be met with resistance, but someone will offer you something you want in the negotiation.

"Storm" 1893

How Someone Sees You

For how someone sees you, this card means the person sees you as someone who doesn't accept neglect or abuse. They know they will have to treat you with respect if they want to hang on to you. They might feel vulnerable as they consider the reality that you may not stay with them.

Future Event or Outcome

As a future event or outcome, someone will decide to walk away from the relationship. They have invested a great deal in this partnership, but upon deeply considering their unhappiness or lack of fulfillment, they will find the courage to walk away

Divining the Art

The woman in this painting runs from the safety of the house during a storm. She no longer trusts the company she keeps, and rather than gather in the comfortable circle of familiar companions, she has taken stock of her situation and has decided she is better off facing her problems alone. Her white dress reflects an innocence: she lacks the life experience to fully understand what is before her on her journey. But the others have turned away from her, suggesting whatever mistakes she feels she has made at some point in the future were unavoidable without a trusted or identified mentor, and that necessary growth lies ahead. Although this tumultuous situation is likely causing you anxiety and grief over what you must leave behind, face this problem head-on. Understand that you need not know everything in advance to move forward with making a critical decision.

Serendipity

9 of Cups

"Budding Leaves" 1911-1915

General Reading:

The nine of cups is a card about harmony and satisfaction. Good luck, or serendipity is on your side, and you can expect to get something you want. Reversed, the card is still positive. You will receive truth in addition to what the card offers upright.

How Someone Sees You

For how someone sees you, this card means you are seen as an ideal person for whatever role you fulfill for them.

Future Event or Outcome

As a future event or outcome in a relationship, expect a serendipitous event to occur! You are in the right place at the right time, and both of you will acknowledge and recognize how the stars have aligned for the two of you.

Divining the Art

This couple basks in each other's company and the beauty of nature surrounding them. It's a happy pairing. The woman's posture suggests she does not have to put on airs for this man; he accepts her as she is and is more interested in her company than any kind of performance. The still waters denotes smooth emotions and peaceful union. This blue sky is all they could have hoped for. Mother Earth has brought them together through divine timing.

Fulfillment

10 of Cups

General Reading:

The Ten of Cups speaks to emotional fulfillment. We are basking in the glory of achieving our heart's desire. This is the card of perfect love and friendship.

If reversed, beware the false heart or violence. Someone is not interested in equality.

How Someone Sees You

For how someone sees you, this card usually means you are not only this person's ideal love, they feel you are stable and a good choice for a life partner. Their perception of you is entirely positive.

Future Event or Outcome

As a future event or outcome in a relationship, you can expect a long term union, since the other person is capable of loving you the way God intended for you to be loved. You can anticipate healthy boundaries, respect, active listening, and affection.

"The Kiss" 1897

Divining the Art

Though this bears some resemblance to the Fate card, notice that our couple is clothed. This detail makes the energy markedly different. Whereas Fate speaks of destiny and soul contracts, the Ten of Cups is less about the spiritual potential of a situation, and more about lasting reality. This couple can connect in the world in a meaningful way. The melding of their faces into one suggests their souls have completely united, and an equal emotional exchange cycles regularly in their relationship. This is not only a couple meant for each other, but a couple who is able to navigate the realities of life together. Meetings are fated, but long term relationships are a choice.

Sensitive Child

Page of Cups

"Bathing Boys" 1904

General Reading:

The Page of Cups in this deck indicates a sensitive child. This could be a literal child in the situation, or if no child applies, then it refers to the sensitivity of childhood that impacts the relationship at this time. This childhood experience makes this person more apt at reflection and self-awareness.

If reversed, be wary of any unhealthy attachment behavior.

How Someone Sees You

For how someone sees you, they see you as sensitive and in need of protection from the outside world. They are aware of the difficulties of your childhood and how those challenges impacted you. You can trust this person to have your best interest at heart.

Divining the Art

The standing boy in this painting is conscious of who is watching, and seems preoccupied with the vulnerability of his nudity. Though the other boys he plays with are also nude, this social normalcy doesn't appear to appease his self-consciousness. He has disconnected from the social activity and withdrawn into his own head. You can expect someone's sensitivity to become the basis for withdrawal and potential conflict if the other partner doesn't make attempts to understand.

Future Event or Outcome

As a future event or outcome in a relationship, expect some news about the other person's past to shed light on the longevity of your relationship. Some part of their psychology will need to be ironed out in order to continue.

Connection

Knight of Cups

"Man and Woman" 1890

General Reading:

In this deck, the Knight of Cups is about romantic connection. This can be the act of sex, but it might also simply mean someone is pursuing someone else with earnest intent and desires such a connection.

If reversed, don't trust what this person claims to be offering you. They are trying to swindle you.

How Someone Sees You

For how someone sees you, this card means they see you as driven and as someone who keeps moving forward until they've achieved what they want. They see you as someone who is clear in their desires and they find this very attractive.

Divining the Art

This intoxicating sketch holds the viewer captive, as they are pulled into this real and fresh sexual encounter. The sparse palette of color seems to be a reflection of the male's perspective, as he sees the situation primitively and perhaps with reduced focus. The energy between the two is inviting and pleasurable. This is the kind of energy that is ripe for fertility, so if kids aren't in the plans right now, use protection.

Future Event or Outcome

As a future event or outcome in a relationship, this card means you can expect a physical union. Whether or not the relationship has staying power is yet to be seen and could go either way.

Intensity

Queen of Cups

General Reading:

The Queen of Cups is generally a kind, loving woman with a lot to offer others emotionally. She is a caretaker and listener. She is honest, devoted, and willing to serve. Her inclination to lead with her heart can make her quite intense at moments.

If reversed, look out for an emotionally unstable woman.

How Someone Sees You

For how someone sees you, they see you as kind and devoted, and also someone who thinks with their heart over their mind. Watch out that this person doesn't intend to take advantage of your goodness or overlooks your intelligence.

Future Event or Outcome

As a future event or outcome in a relationship, expect a woman who matches the Queen of Cups description to appear. Her arrival will bring a change to your situation, though it is unknown whether that change will be for better or worse. Pull two more cards for clarification.

"Tulla Larsen" 1898

Divining the Art

Tulla Larsen was an artist in her own right. She had a four year relationship with Munch and was the only woman he was ever engaged to. She pursued him relentlessly for a commitment, but he continued to evade her, then finally resorted to cruelty to try to stave off her advances. He finally agreed to meet with her after hearing she had become suicidal. Their relationship ended after this meeting, when part of Edvard's finger was shot off. He wouldn't really discuss how this had happened, but created several self-pitying paintings about the aftermath at the hospital later. She was certainly an intense Queen of Cups, offering her love to Munch with fierce tenacity.

Moodiness

King of Cups

General Reading:

The King of Cups is a fair man, composed and kind. He can be trusted, as he has emotional intelligence as well as common sense. He is also adept in business because he engages his instinct. This king can also be overly emotional or moody, since he leads with his heart.

If reversed, this could be a man with mental illness. Beware the drunk.

How Someone Sees You

If someone sees you as the King of Cups, they see you as kind, fair and benevolent. They also feel you possess some kind of mastery that they envy, such as people skills or perhaps a small business with a margin of success. They see you as accomplished as well as having positive qualities.

Future Event or Outcome

As a future event or outcome in a relationship, a man who matches the general description of the King of Cups will enter this situation and play a role in the outcome of this relationship. Pull two more cards for clarification.

"Self-Portrait in Broad-Brimmed Hat" 1906

Divining the Art

Although the King of Cups is sentimental and loving, he can be inclined to moodiness. Artists like Munch were never lacking in their broad range of emotions, and Munch himself struggled with interpersonal relationships throughout his life. At first glance, this face in this painting appears stoic, but the eyes are filled with depth and conflicted feelings. The swirls of paint in the background as well as the red aura painted around the figure indicate spiritual activity that both interferes with and enhances the human experience. Watch out for someone's moodiness. The waters are about to get rocky.

Clarity

Ace of Swords

General Reading:

The Ace of Swords is a card of great force, for better or worse. A truth is typically revealed through the blow this sword delivers. You can expect a tumultuous situation to offer you some clarity.

If reversed, expect an argument.

"The Oak" 1906

How Someone Sees You

For how someone sees you, they see you as a forceful person to be reckoned with. They instinctively know they shouldn't cross you, and they know they can expect to be justly confronted if they disrespect you.

Divining the Art

This painting of an oak tree evokes feelings of longevity and strength. The eye of sunlight peeking through its branches reflects a clear truth revealed that perhaps we have been searching for. The tree's long shadow reminds us that our actions leave a energetic trail of truth in our life, one that carves the path forward. . Notice the blue leaves melding into the sky. What appears distinct and separate can maintains a cosmic interconnectedness through spirit. . This could be a symbol of higher consciousness crossing the barrier into consciousness. Insight can be found if you look for it. The gold hillside surrounding the tree alludes to fortune.

Future Event or Outcome

As a future event or outcome in a relationship, you can expect some kind of breakthrough. Someone finally wraps their head around what they have been doing wrong and begins to offer what they should have in the first place. Or, someone has enough clarity to see this relationship as a dead end and walks away without regrets.

Blind

2 of Swords

General Reading:

The Two of Swords is about both blindness to the external factors that affect a situation, and the idea of being pulled in competing directions as you weigh your own interests against the expectation for you to conform. You are unsure of what to do and grapple with confidence. You don't have a clear picture of your divine worth, or you might be unsure of where your boundaries are, and so you find it impossible to act.

If reversed, then someone else's disloyalty or dishonesty is at the root of this dilemma.

How Someone Sees You

For how someone sees you, they might see you as lacking confidence. They also might see you as someone who can be easily manipulated because they believe you haven't established personal boundaries.

"Vision" 1892

Future Event or Outcome

As a future event or outcome in a relationship, this card means this relationship will eventually test your sense of self. This relationship will be formative to your identity and figuring out what you are willing to put up with from others, and what you are not.

Divining the Art

The asymmetrical eyes of this figure first draws you in: emotional imbalance is the key energy from this painting. Perhaps she has water in her eyes. External factors have affected your ability to see. The clear reflections in the water indicate that insight is available to you as you seek out your innermost feelings and desires. Swans are a symbol of beauty, grace and peace. Take heart: you will sort this puzzle out and calm the inner storm.

Heartbreak

3 of Swords

"Ashes" 1894

General Reading:

The Three of Swords is a card of acute heartbreak. Your emotional pain causes a significant rupture to your daily life.

If reversed, you feel alienated in addition to feeling heartbroken.

How Someone Sees You

With this card, the other person either sees you as someone nursing a heartbreak, or they consider you the cause of their current suffering.

Future Event or Outcome

As a future event or outcome in a relationship, you can expect emotional upheaval. Someone acts in selfishness and causes the other pain.

Divining the Art

Our couple is in obvious turmoil in this composition. He has withdrawn, unable to face the problem, and she is clearly exasperated. Notice the green hues on his face and along one side her dress. These apparent stains give the impression this moment follows an embrace. He appears to be the source of the illness and has tainted her with his psychosis. The forest fades into the blackness of the unknown. Someone in your situation is not willing to face up to the hurt they've caused. Give it time. Even though you are unsure of where you have come from as a couple, and where you are going, focus on the trees you can see along your immediate path for now.

Retreat

4 of Swords

General Reading:

The Four of Swords is a card about rest, recovery, and sometimes grief. We need to withdraw for a bit in order to get over a loss. We will retreat back into our refuge to process our grief, heal physically, or to consider our next move.

If reversed, someone is unwilling to take a risk.

How Someone Sees You

For how someone sees you, they might see you as someone in a stage of recovery from your past. They recognize your need for healing.

"Night in St. Cloud" 1890

Future Event or Outcome

As a future event or outcome in a relationship, one or both of you will need a break from the relationship for a while. However this event is driven by the need to recover, so once recovery has been attained, this relationship might resume. Consider nearby cards.

Divining the Art

This painting depicts a pensive figure gazing out the window to a boat at sea. Notice the reflection of moonlight from the window stretched across the floor. Intuitive answers will lay before you as you go inward and search your soul for the truth. There's a comfort to the darkness that will calm your mind and settle the anxieties that plague you. Though the waters ahead may seem treacherous, your metaphorical ship will arrive in the dark and carry you to safety. Tarry here until you are healed.

Defeat

5 of Swords

"Weeping Nude" 1913

General Reading:

The Five of Swords indicates a conflict where at least one party dominates another. Although it may seem like there is a winner and a loser, this is a lose-lose situation as the victor has had to resort to violence or cruelty to get what they want and this will inevitably backfire. Reversed, the situation includes a final end.

How Someone Sees You

For how someone sees you, this card means they see you as confrontational and as someone who is quick to start conflict.

Future Event or Outcome

As a future event or outcome in a relationship, you can expect a conflict. This card usually means a messy fight, so try to rise above the situation and avoid being the aggressor.

Divining the Art

The figure in this painting certainly feels that she has been on the losing end of a struggle. Her nudity is a reflection of her vulnerability. The positioning of her legs gives off a disheveled energy: she's disoriented and doesn't know whether she is coming or going, sitting or kneeling. The trauma of her situation makes even the most basic of tasks difficult. Note the variety of textures across the back wall. This environment and situation is complex, with many factors at play. Her own shadow above her weighted shoulder morphs into a distinct conglomerate of purple. The uniqueness of one soul shrouded in its own pain reverberates a distinct hue. Your story and its challenges matter greatly within the vast fabric of the universe. Do not diminish the significance of your personal suffering. All souls are great in the sight of God.

Moving Forward

6 of Swords

General Reading:

The Six of Swords marks a journey over water (emotions) away from tumultuous circumstances into more peaceful times. Expect the situation to improve.

If reversed, expect a public declaration of love and perhaps even a wedding proposal.

How Someone Sees You

For how someone sees you, this card means they see you as the key to a path forward. They've been wanting out of their current circumstances and the idea of you provides an exit plan in their mind.

"Boat on the Sea" 1901

Divining the Art

The stones in this painting guide the viewer's eye to the boat in the distance, where a single figure rows across peaceful waters. Your path has been divinely established and the journey to an ideal destination has been set in motion. If you have been struggling through rough times, expect a big break to pull you our of the storm.

Future Event or Outcome

As a future event or outcome in a relationship, you can expect this relationship to move forward with marked improvement in the dynamics between the two of you. Harder times are behind you.

Betrayal

7 of Swords

General Reading:

The Seven of Swords is a card of deception, theft, and betrayal. Someone will attempt to get away with something, but that attempt will fail. This card should not be read as literal death but as the murder of trust.

If reversed, expect slander in the situation.

How Someone Sees You

For how someone sees you, this card would mean they see you as generally dishonest and that they can't accept what you say at face value. They are struggling to trust you.

Future Event or Outcome

As a future event or outcome in a relationship, expect a betrayal of some kind. It can be as innocuous as talking about you behind your back, or as treacherous as cheating. Whatever the situation, the truth is revealed.

Divining the Art

This murder scene depicts a faceless murder victim with blood on his hands. Perhaps this blood denotes his own bad deeds that contributed to this outcome, or perhaps he simply has a blood stained hand from attempting to press against his wound. The walls are dizzying and circular, creating an intoxicating effect that has us questioning our reality. The "murderess" stares ahead emotionless, indicating a senseless and perhaps unprovoked betrayal has occurred. The man's belongings (ashtray, hat, paper, etc.) fill equal space in this composition as the man himself, highlighting the ultimate insignificance of personal possessions. What you believe you have lost in this situation is possibly exaggerated in your mind. You can recover. Don't expect an apology or solace from your abuser.

Obscurity

8 of Swords

General Reading:

The Eight of Swords deals with complexities of self perception and the inability to see a situation clearly. There are barriers and self-restrictions in place that are impeding your progress. External negativity and experiences are factoring heavily in the obscurity you face right now.

If reversed, something unforeseen will dramatically alter the situation you are inquiring about.

How Someone Sees You

For how someone sees you, they would see you as someone who has experienced a lot of hardship in your life, and for that reason you have a difficult time getting your bearings and making personal progress. Note that this may not be necessarily true about you; it's simply what they have gathered through perhaps limited information.

Future Event or Outcome

As a future event or outcome in a relationship, there needs to be some deeper psychological work done by one or both parties in order for this relationship to function on a healthy level. Therapy would be beneficial.

"Woman in Front of a Mirror" 1902

Divining the Art

A woman gazes at her reflection, but the image she sees is obstructed. Perhaps the inaccurate reflection is caused by a faulty mirror, or perhaps her own perceptive lens is what causes the obscurity. Her posture suggests self-consciousness and unease with herself. Someone has probably suggested she wasn't good enough at some point. Spend some time on yourself to sort out what is truly standing in your way of progress.

Anxiety

9 of Swords

General Reading:

The Nine of Swords is about anxiety, disruptive dreams, and general worries. Feelings of despair and an overall sense of failure prevail.

If reversed, your fears are valid and not simply a trick of the mind.

How Someone Sees You

For how someone sees you, this card means they either see you as an anxious person in general, or the thought of you causes them great anxiety.

"The Scream" 1910

Future Event or Outcome

As a future event or outcome in a relationship, this card would mean that one or both of you will spend too much time in their head considering all the ways the relationship could go wrong before it actually does. There is likely great fears of commitment involved.

Divining the Art

This iconic painting is part of the collective subconscious. The facial expression of the central figure captures the psyche of the human condition. Created just after the Victorian era, when decorum was tantamount for navigating socially, I imagine this raw expression of unpleasant emotion provided quite the outlet for its stifled audience. Though whatever is plaguing you may be rooted in unfounded fear, the raw power of what you are feeling is valid. As the pressure within you builds, find a healthy outlet and express yourself.

Destruction
10 of Swords

General Reading:

Generally, the Ten of Swords is about suffering, not necessarily death. As with all tens, we reach the apex of an event, in this case, suffering. The positive aspect to this card is that it marks the start of healing, and the worst is over.

If reversed, expect a fleeting moment of success instead.

"Murder in the Lane" 1919

How Someone Sees You

For how someone sees you, this card means they are aware that you are rising out of a bad situation in your life and healing is your focus right now. This is not necessarily good or bad, simply that they are aware of your personal struggles, likely indicating they are an empathetic person.

Future Event or Outcome

As a future event or outcome in a relationship, you can expect conflict or abuse to reach a culmination. Someone is going to push too far and do damage in the relationship that they won't be able to repair without a great deal of effort.

Divining the Art

What's most ominous about this painting is the body lying in the "lane," its more anthropomorphic qualities absorbed into a lump of death, the victim resembling nothing more than a puddle. The trees almost resemble human figures, silent witnesses to the destruction that has occurred. The culprit is transparent, assuming the ghost like qualities that should belong instead to the victim. If you are processing some emotional pain due to another's cruelty, know that their intentions and true heart are visible to you at this time. Although it may not seem like anyone is watching, the Spirit World is aware of your pain and has set karma in motion for you.

Traumatized Child

Page of Swords

"Two Children Drawing" 1891

General Reading:

The Page of Swords is traditionally a card of vigilance and overseeing. The childhood traumas of the past affect the dynamics of the relationship today.

If reversed, someone might be spying on you.

How Someone Sees You

If someone sees you as the Traumatized Child, they can clearly see how your upbringing and past traumas influence your behavior today. Expect a compassionate friend.

Future Event or Outcome

As a future event or outcome in a relationship, you can expect discussions about your or your partner's past traumas to heal you both and solidify your bond.

Divining the Art

The extraordinary use of light and lines in this painting offers a haunting yet spiritual aspect to an otherwise ordinary scene. One child bends over their art while the other stares openly at their voyeur. It is interesting to note both figures are androgynous. The lines of light in this painting represent the emotional fractures of the child's experience. However, the traumas this child has endured have opened a window through the veil to the Spirit World, and all the comfort and wisdom the Light offers become available through their pain. The embrace of the Divine will extend comfort when called upon. Your traumas can serve yourself and can serve others through your spiritual awakening.

Disconnection

Knight of Swords

"Man and Woman on the Beach" 1907

General Reading:

Generally, the Knight of Swords is a card of opposition and resistance. If this card is not symbolizing an event, it denotes a person who will usually pick a fight.

If reversed, beware of someone without appropriate boundaries.

How Someone Sees You

For how someone sees you, this card means you are seen as high conflict and someone who can be ruthless in an argument.

Future Event or Outcome

As an outcome, this card could mean an argument or fight, but it could also mean that you are with someone who is constantly belittling you and starting conflict, and you will tire of this person's demeanor and cut ties.

Divining the Art

Most distinct in this painting is the haunted look on the man's face. His eyes are vacant, with absent irises and barely visible pupils. He is clearly blind to something. Turned away from the woman, she does not concern him, and he is instead plagued by some distracting thought. The woman stares at the path. She seems hopeful or as though she is waiting for him. It is as though only we, the viewer, see that he is not capable of giving her what she desires. Munch's signature reflected moonlight on the water indicates the presence of the subconscious and the mystical at work. A clear disconnect is troubling you now, but your inner knowing will redeem you.

Honesty

Queen of Swords

General Reading:

The Queen of Swords carries the energy of the sword: yielding truth. This card is about widowhood, divorce, separation and sadness, often the fallout from living one's truth. This card can also represent a woman skilled with the written word. If this description doesn't fit anyone in your life, then this queen can represent an event that will cause a change.

If reversed, watch out for a malicious and deceitful woman.

How Someone Sees You

For how someone sees you, this card might mean they view you primarily through your marital status, particularly if you are widowed, divorced, or just leaving a long relationship. They likely view you as honest and not someone who puts up appearances or wears a fake smile.

"Eva Mudocci" ~Unknown

Future Event or Outcome

As a future event or outcome in a relationship, this card could indicate separation or divorce, but often it simply means someone is finally honest and this honesty causes a shift in the relationship. At last, the truth comes out, and the sting of truth creates a boundary that is not easily crossed once it has been laid.

Divining the Art

This painting has a fascinating narrative, as it wasn't attributed to Edvard Munch until 2018. This painting hung in a museum at St. Olaf College in Northfield, Minnesota for 20 years before someone thought it might be Munch's work. Forensic scientists were able to match the paint to some of Munch's other pieces during the period he associated with Eva, and the painting is widely believed to be his. His relationship with Eva was complicated, as she was already in a relationship with a woman when they met. Her sharp intellect and her non-traditional marital status make Eva Mudocci a nice fit for the Queen of Swords, someone who lived honest and true to herself.

Intellectual

King of Swords

General Reading:

The King of Swords roots himself in the idea of justice, particularly how it is bestowed in the courtroom; he can represent a lawyer, or perhaps someone who is quite talented at persuasion or the written word. This king is well read and intellectual in nature, with a superior ability to reason.

If reversed, beware of someone manipulative and with cunning but evil intentions.

How Someone Sees You

For how someone sees you, this card means they see you as well-spoken, articulate, and someone who is interested in politics or government. Your passion for justice extends beyond the dichotomy of right and wrong.

"Hands in Pockets" 1925

Future Event or Outcome

As a future event or outcome in a relationship, you can expect one party to make a grand power play, possibly exercising their right to involve local authorities or the justice system in order to get what they want.

Divining the Art

The face of the figure in this painting is obscured, his more human qualities less noticeable than his posture and stance. The bookcase behind him represents all the books this educated man has read. His shadow expands into something greater than himself, obstructing the view of the bookcase and hovering quite hauntingly over the figure. The hand in the pocket denotes self-assurance, but his towering shadow leads us to believe everything about him cannot be gleaned from his own presentation. Though distractingly intelligent and well composed, he has decided to keep secrets for now. The shadow of his secrets can be perceived, however, by the intent observer.

Passion

Ace of Wands

General Reading:

The Ace of Wands is about the potential of passion within one's life. This can be a symbol of fertility or creativity. A manifestation from the Spirit World wants to emerge on the earth plane, and it needs your help.

If reversed, expect the passion with someone to die far too quickly to make the initial investment worth your time.

How Someone Sees You

For how someone sees you, this card would mean they see you as driven, passionate and creative. You have great ideas and they find this infectious and desire to be around you.

Future Event or Outcome

As a future event or outcome in a relationship, aces don't generally give us concrete details. Instead, they speak of potential, and so the Ace of Wands would mean there is a good fire burning here, but the outcome is unforeseen at this time and largely depends on the choices of the couple.

"View from Nordstrad" 1900

Divining the Art

Consider the metaphor of the flaming tree, which will be forever transformed by its fire, but whose light and heat will be felt for a glorious moment. The trunks of the nearby trees nearly form a warrior figure, raising a victorious spear. Do not fear the moment when the fire fades and the glory dies. There will be other moments like these. Chase this idea, this passion, this connection wherever it will lead you. Pursuing passion is what life is all about.

Discussion

2 of Wands

General Reading:

The Two of Wands is generally about planning, reflection and considering your next move. In a relationship, this could indicate a discussion where both parties are trying to ascertain whether they make sense as a couple.

If reversed, expect a surprise to thwart your expectations.

How Someone Sees You

For how someone sees you, this card would mean that they are still trying to decide how they feel about you, and that they have a wide range of feelings that they are attempting to reconcile.

Future Event or Outcome

As a future event or outcome in a relationship, this card would mean if you are afraid this relationship might be over, take heart. You will have at least one significant discussion before making a final decision. Even if it seems over for now, expect communication.

"Eye in Eye" 1894

Divining the Art

The two figures in this painting are both sad. Neither is getting their needs met in this relationship, even if the turmoil is simply caused by one partner not being willing to invest. These two are at eye level with each other, so you can expect an honest exchange without games from this person. The shadows in the painting overtake the landscape. Don't allow your unhappiness in this relationship eclipse the other aspects of your life. You will find a way to sort it out and move forward, so don't allow this unhappiness to define your state of being.

Jealousy

3 of Wands

General Reading:

The Three of Wands is traditionally a card about the successful return on investments. In this deck, however, the "investment" is putting energy into another person, and the "return" is the formation of an awkward love triangle.

If reversed, this love triangle will end without a dramatic fallout.

"Jealousy" 1913

How Someone Sees You

For how someone sees you, this card would mean they are generally jealous of you or about you. They might envy what you have or feel your level of attractiveness is greater than their own. Or, they might feel jealous and possessive about you, threatened by your other potential suitors.

Future Event or Outcome

As a future event or outcome in a relationship, expect jealousy to be at the heart of key events that determine the future for the two of you.

Divining the Art

I suppose we can guess the figure on the left is green with envy, though the other man in this painting has a sickly yellow-green hue as well. It is our full-faced man who seems to be the center of emotional turmoil here, however. The other man looks down, clearly uncomfortable but not quite angry. Perhaps a rivalry has them both thrown off balance. The woman is red-faced with primitive facial features. Her guilt is apparent, and her humanity has been diminished to an apparition. The posturing of her arms raises questions as well: is she smug over the men fighting over her? Or is she relaxing, free of strife since she is not part of the competition? Either way, expect a love triangle to emerge. One party will be more intensely jealous than the other, and whoever is at the center better take action and decide or will risk losing both.

Celebration

4 of Wands

General Reading:

The Four of Wands is a card of stability and celebration, often depicting a wedding scene. This is the card of harmony, refuge, repose and peace.

If reversed, include prosperity as well.

"Dance on the Shore" ~1900

How Someone Sees You

For how someone sees you, this card means you are the person they wish to celebrate life with. They see you as a permanent fixture in their life, and they undoubtedly love you. They likely see you as family.

Future Event or Outcome

As a future event or outcome in a relationship, expect a public celebration. This could be a formal wedding, or it might be a grand event you attend together where powerful memories are formed.

Divining the Art

The rich array of color and clear whimsy of this painting offers us a dreamy escape from the real world. The dancing figures on the shore denote free-willed fun and nostalgia. The dog sprinting in the corner of this scene adds to the carefree charm of the composition. A salmon-colored moon taints the clouds and its reflection skips across the waves. This is a time of celebration and feeling comfortable with your station in life. There are actually five figures in this painting: two in black are standing not far from the dancers, most likely indicative of older women, and a figure shrouded in red sits and watches the scene. Where are you in this painting? Are you observing, monitoring, or in the heart of the excitement?

Conflict

5 of Wands

"Man and Woman" 1898

General Reading:

The Five of Wands is a card about competing interests. You want something, the other party wants something, and these two ideas do not mesh. This is usually resolved through discussion. If reversed, expect litigation or a dispute.

How Someone Sees You

For how someone sees you, this card means they see you as wanting a different life than they want.

Future Event or Outcome

As a future event or outcome in a relationship, this card indicates some kind of conflict will arise. The resulting argument is usually dramatized more than what the situation warrants. You can expect this to blow over and be reconciled through discussion, given surrounding cards do not indicate an end.

Divining the Art

The nudity in this painting is anything but sexual. It's as though her sexual potential taunts or tortures him in some way. He is clearly overwhelmed with emotion. Her disfigured face and matching red veil are both haunting and ominous. She can no longer speak and be heard. Her desire for wedded union seems laced with malice or ill intentions. The black shadow against the wall overtakes the backdrop of the painting. They are both about to be swallowed by the shared negativity in this relationship. Notice the texture of gold on the wall resembling wings. Perhaps if they shine the light there, the darkness could be tamed. This painting hints at discord caused by someone wanting a commitment that the other party doesn't feel ready for.

Victory
6 of Wands

General Reading:

The Six of Wands is a card of triumph, victory, or exciting news. In a relationship, two parties have figured out how to respect and honor one another for a successful long-term dynamic.

If reversed, the card represents fear and apprehension.

"Summer Night in Studenterlund" 1899

How Someone Sees You

For how someone sees you, this card means they see you as a positive influence for their life and someone they feel they can "win at life" with.

Future Event or Outcome

As a future event or outcome in a relationship, this card means any struggles or conflicts will be sorted out and overcome in your relationship so you can move forward together. If you are single, expect "the one" to arrive.

Divining the Art

Several couples embrace in a public park beneath a perfectly blue sky. All is right with the world, and we want to shout the joy of our relationship from the rooftop and display it publicly. The purple shrubbery have a fantastical quality: the world is seen with rose-colored glasses for now. Note the tall precipice of trees. Embrace this moment in time with all its natural power and glory.

Evasion

7 of Wands

General Reading:

The Seven of Wands is a card of conflict in which you have some kind of advantage against the other party. You will be able to successfully evade their attempts to control or possess you.

If reversed, this card is a warning not to be too indecisive.

How Someone Sees You

For how someone sees you, this card means they are intimidated by you.

Future Event or Outcome

As a future event or outcome in a relationship, you can expect a conflict or confrontation, but you won't be vulnerable during this dispute. You have the ability to manage the situation to your benefit.

Divining the Art

This painting comes from a series that depicts scenes from inside a brothel, so we can presume the female figure here is a prostitute. The man is clearly making her uncomfortable, and she looks as though she would like to escape. The busy wallpaper pattern is dizzying and creates the feeling of claustrophobia. The situation you are in right now is uncomfortable and you might feel vulnerable and scared. But you have the resources and wits to pull yourself out of this situation and evade someone else's selfish intentions towards you. Believe in your own strength and valor and you will emerge the victor.

Message

8 of Wands

"Conversation" 1917

General Reading:

The Eight of Wands is the card of swift energy, such as a message, and also represents the arrows of love. This is a positive card, and its message delivers good news.

If reversed, it can mean jealousy, quarrels, and domestic disputes.

How Someone Sees You

For how someone sees you, this card means you are communicative and someone they like to talk to. They see you as romantic and energetic.

Future Event or Outcome

As a future event or outcome in a relationship, if the dynamic between you has been lackluster lately, you can expect this to change through positive communication. If you haven't heard from someone in a while, you can expect that phone call or text.

Divining the Art

Two women link arms in a moment of shared intimacy. By the brunette's expression, it appears some kind of healing is needed, and the other woman offers some comfort or solace in this situation. The blond's nudity does not seem sexual but rather honest. She is willing to be vulnerable as a means of providing healing. Her blue skirt extends across the bed as though the layers of society and its restrictions can be discarded so to consider the naked truth of the situation. You can expect a communication and connection that is rooted in truth and honesty.

Stuck

9 of Wands

General Reading:

The Nine of Wands is a card of battlement, and it means strength in opposition. You might feel stuck for now, but you have the strength and power to successfully fight your adversary. In a relationship, the problem might be an issue the two of you have, or your partner might be so adversarial that you need to leave.

If reversed, expect a large obstacle before victory.

How Someone Sees You

For how someone sees you, this card means they see you as defensive and that you preemptively expect to be attacked. This is likely due to mistreatment you've experienced in the past that has caused you to rightfully learn that people can't always be trusted.

Future Event or Outcome

As a future event or outcome in a relationship, this card means you will eventually feel stuck in your situation and this will continue for a while before you are able to overcome the issue. If you've been considering leaving, you will likely take more time to ponder and prepare before taking action. This card is a reminder that you do have the power to remove yourself from a situation that doesn't nurture you.

"The Hands" 1893

Divining the Art

A woman stands comfortably while surrounded by multicolored, disembodied hands. They seem to represent the greed and desire of others, though she maintains a safe distance from their grasp. Her black shadow is almost an invisible barrier that protects her, as though she has cast some kind of spiritual protection against the adversarial forces that would consume her. One nipple is more prominent than the other, though she stands evenly with this imbalance. Her expression is unhappy, but not intimidated or afraid. You will get through this.

Overwhelmed

10 of Wands

General Reading:

The Ten of Wands is a card of oppression and a warning that the emotional burdens you carry have the potential to transform into your own oppressive actions towards others if you don't maintain self-awareness.

If reversed, the card acknowledges external difficulties outside your control that contribute to your feeling overwhelmed.

How Someone Sees You

For how someone sees you, they might see you as depressed or as someone in a situation where they are up against a lot of stress and barriers. They likely do not see your depression as an extension of your personality, but rather see the circumstances and events that have contributed to your mental state.

Future Event or Outcome

As a future event or outcome in a relationship, this card means the relationship bears many burdens and there is more than one problem affecting the quality of this relationship. It will be difficult to heal these troubles with so many complex issues.

"Seated Nude with Three Male Heads" 1895-98

Divining the Art

A shapeless nude girl gazes at three floating heads. Disembodied hands are outstretched at her feet. This painting is a nightmare of the subconscious. The three heads represent various voices competing for attention. One looks angry, one disengaged, and one open and welcoming. The flat-chested girl appears prepubescent, suggesting naivety in her perception of what's before her. The outstretched hands might offer her some refuge, but they are difficult to spot while three giant heads swim at eye level. They appear to be attached to a green vine, not fully human forms but instead representative of ideas and distressing thoughts. It is the mind that plagues her. If you are feeling overwhelmed, try reaching out to someone more experienced than yourself for advice on how to approach what is troubling you.

Adventurous Child

Page of Wands

"Boat with Three Boys" 1886

General Reading:

The Page of Wands is the card of the faithful lover. He/She might be somewhat elusive, but honest. His/Her sense of adventure and childlike enthusiasm is what makes him/her attractive.

If reversed, it can mean indecision and instability.

How Someone Sees You

For how someone sees you, they see you as an adventurous person who likes to explore, socialize and travel. You get restless and bored and seek out new experiences. You haven't lost your childlike enthusiasm for the world.

Future Event or Outcome

As a future event or outcome in a relationship, this card means a common need for adventure will solidify the bond between you. One or both of you has not allowed the harsh messages of the world to kill your optimism in life. You will explore together and grow closer through your shared experience.

Divining the Art

A small boy leans over the edge of a boat precariously as two other boys stand and steer. Although the older boys are set on controlling their destiny and steering their boat (quite literally) the younger boy is comfortable allowing others to worry about direction and instead gazes mesmerized at the passing water. A need to connect to nature and a natural willingness to cast off troubles guides this boy's behavior. Set your worries aside and let others ponder them for a while. Connect to what is around you and let its natural magic fortify your experience.

Pursuit

Knight of Wands

"The Lonely Ones" 1935

General Reading:

The Knight of Wands is the card of an errand. This Knight is on a mission. In a relationship, it can refer to someone who is intent on wooing someone else, and pursues them with great energy.

If reversed, expect someone to quickly depart.

How Someone Sees You

For how someone sees you, they see you as someone with intentions. You have made what you want clear and have established an expectation with them. They appreciate your straightforwardness and that they don't have to guess what you're thinking.

Future Event or Outcome

As a future event or outcome in a relationship, one of you is going to heavily pursue the other, perhaps to the point of tiring them or wearing them down. Whether or not the other party will relent and agree to a relationship is yet to be determined.

Divining the Art

Munch painted "The Lonely Ones" in many various versions. The title leads us to believe this couple is not yet together, yet the man is moving toward the woman, intent on communicating with her and probably making an attempt to connect. The unnatural purple of the sky leads us to believe he might have some unrealistic expectations concerning this relationship and what it will offer. Her side of the sky is blue, but is almost the same color as the water, indicating her view of the world might be more realistic, but has drained life of its magnetism by being too pragmatic. The landscape before the shore nearly comes alive in its haphazard and unnatural shapes. Emotions are running high, and neither party feels settled at the moment. Are you the pursuer or the one being pursued?

Vivacious

Queen of Wands

General Reading:

The Queen of Wands is generally a woman with a vibrant personality, social, likable and often the center of attention. As a symbol, she would represent a good time. She is often physically attractive

If reversed, she represents infidelity or the "other woman"

How Someone Sees You

For how someone sees you, they see you as social, honorable, vibrant and fun. It's also likely they find you physically attractive. You are seen as a vivacious person and someone they want to be around. They value their association with you because they feel it heightens their own social status.

"Ingse" 1903

Future Event or Outcome

As a future event or outcome in a relationship, this card means expect to meet someone special at a public event. If you are paired with someone, this means your partner will plan a public outing with you that will impress your circle of friends.

Divining the Art

Ingse was an acquaintance and long time pen-pal to Munch. She leaned over his fence one day to chat, which inspired this painting. She often sent him funny and flirtatious postcards, and it was clear she her friendly and social demeanor kept Munch interested in her adventures long after they had parted ways.

Artist

King of Wands

General Reading:

The King of Wands is an honest, friendly and generally married man. This card has a reputation of being associated with the arts and leadership as well. If reversed, this card represents a very strict man.

How Someone Sees You

For how someone sees you, this card means you are seen as artistic, a natural leader, creative and diplomatic. They see you as having reached a phase of accomplishment with your talents and they hold a great deal of respect for you.

"Self-portrait with Brushes" 1904

Divining the Art

This self-portrait as artist captures the King of Wands nicely. As an icon in his field, Munch definitely embodies the great sense of accomplishment and mastery that king energy embodies. The straight brushes in his hand reflect focus and singularity in task. Expect to engage with someone who considers themselves a creator and takes this work seriously.

Future Event or Outcome

As a future event or outcome in a relationship, this card means you will reach a comfortable and honest level in your relationship. This connection definitely has the potential to go the distance.

Security

Ace of Pentacles

"Shore with Red House" 1904

General Reading:

The Ace of Pentacles speaks to the potential of the material world. The possibility for wealth and abundance is reflected in this card. This is also the card of contentment.

If reversed, it indicates corruption through riches.

How Someone Sees You

For how someone sees you, this card means they see great potential in you to manifest your dreams.

Future Event or Outcome

As a future event or outcome in a relationship, you can expect your relationship to progress in a concrete way, including moving in together, sharing resources and building wealth together.

Divining the Art

The romantic setting of this painting evokes feelings of comfort and aesthetic appreciation. The connection between material world and the spiritual world is represented in the building, rocks, and the expanse of sea. The primary view in this painting is of the stones, grounding us to the earth and urging us to appreciate the small details of nature. The scene equally captures the glory of Mother Nature and the comforts of what we call home. These earthly materials are here for you to enjoy and augment the beauty of your life.

Exchange

2 of Pentacles

"Red and White" 1899-1900

General Reading:

The Two of Pentacles encompasses a juggling energy. Energy flows in while energy flows out. For a relationship, the card may mean trading one partner for another.

If reversed, expect a text exchange.

How Someone Sees You

For how someone sees you, this card means they see you as a good communicator and someone with good judgment.

Future Event or Outcome

As a future event or outcome in a relationship, this card means you can expect some aspect of the relationship to change. This could mean a new home or new job that impacts the relationship significantly, or someone might decide to change partners.

Divining the Art

The composition of this painting includes two women standing perpendicular to each other as though they are on an invisible rotation. The woman in white seems to represent someone unreachable, while the woman in red is present and accessible. Beware of someone who focuses on what they can't have and makes relationship decisions based on their ego. Look for the person who recognizes and appreciates what is before them, who discards what the world tells them to value, and instead focuses on the beauty and uniqueness of the individual. This is the person who is worth your investment. You need someone willing to journey into the forest of the unknown with you, not someone who looks to the sea without a boat to traverse those great waters. Don't internalize another's lack of wisdom. Their need to grow is not a reflection of your worth.

Complete

3 of Pentacles

General Reading:

The Three of Pentacles is a card of collaboration and teamwork. This card typically denotes the successful completion of a goal. In a relationship, this would refer to the successful completion of a shared goal, perhaps financial or interpersonal, likely including the help of a third party such as a professional advisor or therapist.

If reversed, the outcome of the goal will be weak or mediocre. Therapy won't cause much to change.

How Someone Sees You

For how someone sees you, they see you as goal-oriented and hard working. They also see you as a team player.

Future Event or Outcome

As a future event or outcome in a relationship, this card is a good omen that points to productivity, harmony and accomplishment. You have the ability to successfully manage life together. This card does not tell us, however, whether you will find emotional fulfillment through this arrangement.

"Spring in Dr. Linde's Garden" 1903

Divining the Art

Three figures lay in the grass. They appear to be resting after a leisure activity, the butterfly net offering some clue of what they have been up to. Their close proximity to one another in such a wide, open space indicates the close bond they share and the harmony that facilitates their union. These three are comfortable together, and their warmth of their fraternizing offers a sense of completion. The surreal blue tree offers feelings of whimsy and a carefree connection with nature. All is well.

Control

4 of Pentacles

"Cupid and Psyche" 1907

General Reading:

The Four of Pentacles is basically about possessiveness, often referring to money but can include possessiveness towards another as well.

If reversed, expect a delay to something promised.

How Someone Sees You

For how someone sees you, they might see you as generally controlling. This could be interpersonally or financially.

Future Event or Outcome

As a future event or outcome in a relationship, this card means this relationship will becoming stifling if it isn't already. Expect to have your freedoms reduced and your needs and feelings minimized in the interest of your partner.

Divining the Art

The myth of Cupid and Psyche is that Psyche (a human princess) was so beautiful that jealous Venus sent her son Cupid to meddle in her love affairs. Instead, Cupid falls in love with her and convinces her to marry him, but he hides his godhood from her, only visiting her at night. One night, she finally lights a lamp and discovers his godliness, and that is the moment represented here. Notice the lines across their bodies like prison bars. Instead of angelic, Cupid looks dark and unremarkable. And Psyche, supposedly the most beautiful woman in the world, looks sleep-deprived and quite lackluster. Munch seemed to reject the idea that these two abstract beings (Love=Cupid and the Mind=Psyche) could have romance. Instead, we are left with Cupid standing somewhat menacingly over the object of his affections. Sometimes another's possessiveness looks like love, but serves only their ego.

Loss

5 of Pentacles

"Crouching Nude" 1917-1919

General Reading:

The Five of Pentacles is a card of loss, particularly financial loss, but in a relationship reading, it would be interpreted as the loss of connection.

If reversed, this loss includes chaos and disorder.

How Someone Sees You

For how someone sees you, this card usually means you are seen as poor, either in material wealth or in spirit, or both.

Future Event or Outcome

As a future event or outcome in a relationship, this does not bode well for the longevity of the connection. Imbalance will affect your ability to sustain a relationship. This imbalance could be caused by outside forces, or by personal issues.

Divining the Art

A nude woman lays in the fetal position across a red sofa. Her facial features are harshly and crudely realized, suggesting her emotional state is so severe that she lacks clarity in her life. Her nudity is not sexual and is instead an extension of emotional vulnerability. She has laid it all out for someone else, and has been abandoned or left wanting. It will take some time to process and cope with this disappointment. Comfort remains elusive for now. Give it time as you meditate and center yourself. You will pass through this.

Apology

6 of Pentacles

"Under the Stars" 1900-1905

General Reading:

The Six of Pentacles is a card about charity, gifts, gratification and attention. In a relationship reading, this can manifest as an apology, as someone is charitable in spirit and gives you what you need to move forward.

If reversed, expect jealousy and/or resentment to remain despite the apology

How Someone Sees You

For how someone sees you, this card usually means you are seen as naive or perhaps and adventurous.

Future Event or Outcome

As a future event or outcome in a relationship, this card means someone will bend in a conflict and make efforts to amend the discord between you.

Divining the Art

A man buries his head in the bosom of a woman across a bloody path. She embraces him lovingly, though her skull-like face offers a haunting perspective. What has he killed in her? It's clear she is not ready to walk away just yet. The lights in the houses of the background hint that knowledge and refuge could be offered elsewhere, were she to turn around. A night sky smoldering with green suggests the heavenly realm and the earthly plane are in symbiotic connection. Tonight, under the stars, the veil to the other side is thin, and spiritual knowledge is accessible. Look to astrology charts for insight at this time.

Longing

7 of Pentacles

General Reading:

The Seven of Pentacles is a card of planting and waiting for crops to sprout and provide harvest, so it is often a card of waiting and patience. In a relationship reading, it refers to waiting for a lover or partner to come back into our lives. Your soul is purified during this wait.

If reversed, expect an extra long wait.

"Flower of Pain" 1897

How Someone Sees You

For how someone sees you, this card means they feel they must wait to have you. Or alternatively, it could mean that they feel you are worth their investment.

Future Event or Outcome

As a future event or outcome in a relationship, this card means a time of separation while one or both parties must grow in order to fully understand and appreciate the beauty that this particular relationship adds to their life.

Divining the Art

A man's broken heart bleeds down his body into the earth, and a large white flower similar to a calla lily springs from this pain. A blood colored sky taints an otherwise bleak composition. This man is consumed by his own pain and shows little interest in the surrounding world. His own suffering is the most poignant aspect of his existence. He does not look up to appreciate the beauty of the flower that has arisen from this pain. If you are left wanting from a relationship, consider what is slowly growing in your interior landscape as you learn to process this hardship. Your sorrow, longing and sadness does not stay in your body nor does it evaporate into the abyss. Instead, it finds fertile ground in your path, where it can appropriately thrive. Trust in your mind and heart's natural ability to plant seeds in your life.

Work

8 of Pentacles

"Worker and Child" 1908

General Reading:

The Eight of Pentacles is the card of apprenticeship and work. In a relationship, it refers to the team effort and hard work invested in making that relationship successful and mutually beneficial.

If reversed, expect someone to say they will work on issues, but not follow through.

How Someone Sees You

For how someone sees you, this card means they see you as ambitious and dedicated.

Future Event or Outcome

As a future event or outcome in a relationship, this card means that the relationship needs work in order to be successful. It's a good indicator that the two of you have a vested interest in putting in the time to improve the relationship.

Divining the Art

This charming scene depicts a man breaking a line formation of workers in order to embrace a child. The pink road contrasts starkly against the disheveled and dirty workers. We can assume this is his daughter, perhaps hugging him before a long day's work. His assimilated uniform to the group reflects his dedication to his community and his commitment to his employer, but he hasn't forgotten what is important in life. This card urges you to work hard, but not to lose sight of what is really important in life. Your true path is like a child with its arms outstretched: you might overlook it or dismiss its needs if you prioritize your standing in the world.

Independence

9 of Pentacles

"Girl Under the Apple Tree" 1904

General Reading:

The Nine of Pentacles is a card of independence and accomplishment, as well as prudence and safety. In a relationship reading, this card means you have the ability to meet your own needs and therefore, you are in a position to be selective about your romantic partners. This card often appears when you are in a relationship that doesn't serve you, when are trying to decide about a potential partner, or when you are single and not feeling very happy about it. Remember you are in a position of power.

If reversed, someone is trying to convince you that you aren't empowered, based on untruth.

How Someone Sees You

For how someone sees you, this card usually means they see you as self-sufficient and successful. This is probably an ideal card for how someone sees you because they will be compelled to respect you.

Future Event or Outcome

As a future event or outcome in a relationship, this card has a couple possible interpretations. This card might be urging you to cut off a toxic person and become more self reliant. It might be forecasting a fantastic single phase in your life if you are already single. Sometimes it can mean you will experience financial gains that would possibly make you independent, and will inevitably rock the boat of your relationship, even if you have no intention of leaving because it will provoke their insecurities. This card is positive and does not indicate the end of a relationship necessarily. Instead, it reminds you that you have choices.

Divining the Art

A woman stands erect before an apple tree on a beautiful estate. The greenery surround her symbolizing her riches. Dressed conservatively, she holds a withdrawn expression, casually grasping plucked flowers from the garden. No one has access to her unless she desires their intrusion. The shrubbery wall before the house closes us off to the material world and connects us to our natural state. You are not putting on airs to impress others, yet you impress them anyway. You will thrive in this environment and success will be yours.

Attainment

10 of Pentacles

"Apple Tree in the Garden" 1932-1942

General Reading:

The Ten of Pentacles is the card of gain, riches, and family abode. For a relationship it would indicate settling down and sharing a domestic life together, and includes wealth in addition to emotional harmony. For a relationship reading, this might be as good as it gets if security and commitment are part of your value system.

If reversed, this foretells of an unexpected dowry, inheritance or pension.

How Someone Sees You

For how someone sees you, this card would mean they consider your presence their literal home. They are likely to value their relationship with you over their worldly possessions because you are their world.

Future Event or Outcome

As a future event or outcome in a relationship, this card means prosperity in domestic life together. If you're wondering if this relationship will last, you can put those worries to rest.

Divining the Art

The abundance of apples in this painting represents the wealth you have accumulated in your life thus far. The unnatural blue of the shrubbery branches remind you that otherworldly forces such as ancestors or guides have helped you acquire the worldly possessions you have gathered. The yellow house's position atop a hill indicates you have achieved a level of attainment above others. The windblown shrub near the house tells us you've weathered some storms and come out on the other side victorious. Family waits for you inside your charming home, and the bright blue of the sky forecasts a lengthy period of prosperity in your life.

Needy Child

Page of Pentacles

"The Magic Forest" 1919

General Reading:

The Page of Pentacles is generally a card of application of knowledge. In this deck, we present the Needy Child, whose unmet needs have a marked impact on the psychology of one or both parties in a relationship. This card is an insight into what might truly be the problem, and provides a key to a solution.

If reversed, someone is struggling to see this issue clearly.

How Someone Sees You

For how someone sees you, this card usually means they're not willing to validate your needs.

Future Event or Outcome

As a future event or outcome in a relationship, this card means unmet needs in childhood will exacerbate relationship problems in the future.

Divining the Art

A transparent mother and child cross a windy path in this captivating composition. The barren, disheveled trees create a lost and hopeless tone. The transparency of the human figures leads us to question their physical existence. Are these spirits or figments of the imagination? The trees of the path close in on the viewer, creating a feeling of claustrophobia and disorientation. The situation appears treacherous and threatening, but perhaps it is simply our perception and tendency to look for portentous signs that is the real problem. Look to the experiences of your past, particularly your childhood, to sort the truth from the fear.

Arrival

Knight of Pentacles

"Adam and Eve" 1928

General Reading:

The Knight of Pentacles is the card of permanency. You can expect someone to show up and remain in your life.

If reversed, you might have trouble getting rid of this person.

How Someone Sees You

For how someone sees you, they see you as dependable and don't believe you would abandon them.

Future Event or Outcome

As a future event or outcome in a relationship, this card means the relationship will not be fleeting but will endure for a considerable amount of time. This relationship will leave an indelible mark in your life whether it endures or ends.

Divining the Art

A romantic scene beneath an apple tree presents a man and woman engaged in conversation. She is casually eating, at ease with his presence. We get the impression this relationship is in its formation stage. The male attempts an aloof posturing, one hand in his pocket, though his arm outstretched over the tree towards her gives away his true feelings. The blue sky peaking through the orchard continues nearly down the height of the composition, creating a bit of disorientation. Prepare to have your world turned upside down by this chance meeting. This will be a relationship for the books.

Nurturing

Queen of Pentacles

General Reading:

The Queen of Pentacles is an intelligent, earthy woman. Sometimes she is pregnant or a mother. Occasionally, she possesses intuitive gifts. She is often seen as nurturing, and the bedrock of her family unit.

If reversed, beware an evil woman who uses her usefulness to manipulate others.

"Birgit Prestøe in the Garden" 1924-1930

How Someone Sees You

For how someone sees you, this card means you are the heart of your home and others depend on your stability for their own psychological health. This person perceives you as the rock that you are.

Future Event or Outcome

As a future event or outcome in a relationship, this card means indicates warmth and stability in a relationship. Expect to feel appreciated and a to enjoy a strong sense of purpose in this partnership.

Divining the Art

The woman in this painting seems to almost morph into her environment. The trees and garden are almost painted around her rather than composed as part of one continuous vision. It could be the green spiritual halo painted around her that seems to divide the subjects. Her natural spirituality is of the earth. Nature bends to her will. The light in the distance indicates the spiritual insight within her grasp. The obscure patches of yellow and green within the garden show us that her essence holds the power to alter her environment. This is a powerful woman, but if you don't value the inherent power of nature, you will foolishly overlook her magnitude.

Dependability

King of Pentacles

"Self-portrait Against a Blue Sky" 1908

General Reading:

The King of Pentacles is a master of business, valor, and mathematical aptitude. He gathers the material world in his hands and makes the most from it. Whereas the Queen of Pentacles works with nature, the King dominates it, but will take measures to replenish that which he consumes when upright.

If reversed, this card indicates a man who would exploit nature for financial gain.

How Someone Sees You

For how someone sees you, they see you as having keen business sense and strong project management skills.

Future Event or Outcome

As a future event or outcome in a relationship, expect the King of Pentacles to appear and change your situation. If he's a symbol, financial gains will rock your relationship for better or worse.

Divining the Art

This outdoor self portrait was painted when Munch was around forty-five years old. He seems content and noticeably without angst in this portrayal, and the sky molds around his head as though the great world is ready to make room for him. The grass placed at shoulder level appears to support his stature. The clouds in the sky indicate that perhaps all in this man's life is not ideal at this time, yet the brisk yellow of his shirt and the crispness of his jacket present a man ready to face and mold the world at large. Expect to meet someone coming out of trouble, but who has emerged from reflection and feels ready to tackle his situation and make permanent choices for their life..

Made in United States
North Haven, CT
19 October 2022

25654319R00049